SB2U Vindicator in action

By Tom Doll
Color by Don Greer
Illustrated by Joe Sewell

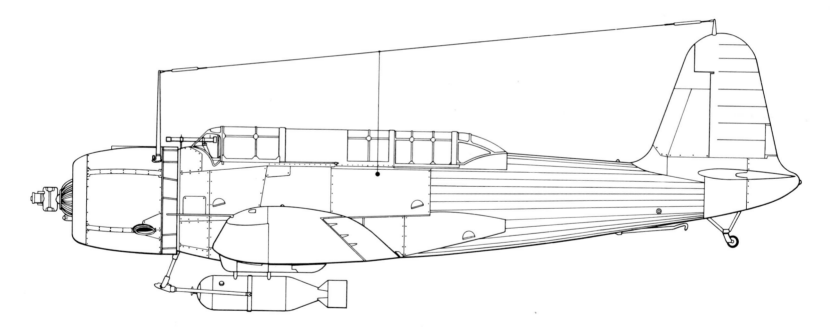

Aircraft Number 122
squadron/signal publications

On 4 June 1942, Marine SB2U-3 Vindicators of VMSB-241 based on Midway Island attacked the Japanese battleship HARUNA. Aircraft #6 was flown by 2LT James H. Marmande and his rear seat gunner was PFC Ed Colvin.

ISBN 0-89747-274-8

If you have any photographs of the aircraft, armor, soldiers or ships of any nation, particularly wartime snapshots, why not share them with us and help make Squadron/Signal's books all the more interesting and complete in the future. Any photograph sent to us will be copied and the original returned. The donor will be fully credited for any photos used. Please send them to:

Squadron/Signal Publications, Inc.
1115 Crowley Drive.
Carrollton, TX 75011-5010.

Dedication

To the happy memory of David H. Stricker, loving husband, responsible father and gentle friend — one of the most courageous men I have ever known. Dave's cheerful heart and positive attitude never wavered even as the days grew dark. I shall always miss him.

Acknowledgements

I wish to express a sincere "thank you" to the following groups and individuals in recognition of their generosity in helping to compile the photographs and information in this book.

Geoffrey Bussy
MAJ John M. Elliott, USMC (Ret)
Berkley R. Jackson
William T. Larkins
William A. Riley
David H. Stricker
United States Marine Corps
United Technologies Archives
Joseph H. Weathers, Jr.
National Archives & Records Center

Robert J. Cressman
Harry Gann
Clay Jansson
Musee de l'Air
Art Schoeni
William L. Swisher
United States Navy
D. Bruce Van Alstine
MSGT Walter F. Gemeinhardt, USMC (Ret)
Peter M. Bowers

This SB2U-1, 3-B-14, in flight over the San Joaquin Valley during May of 1939, was the second aircraft in Section Five of VB-3. The aircraft is carrying a 50 gallon drop tank on the centerline bomb rack. (Navy)

U.S.NAVY
3-B-14

3

Introduction

The Vought SB2U series of scout bombers was manufactured between 1936 and 1941 for both the United States Navy and Marine Corps. When these aircraft were first introduced they represented a major transition from the biplane to the modern low wing monoplane. The Vought entry in the Navy Bureau of Aeronautics 1934 design competition featured a number of new innovative ideas as well as a number of features "carried over" from the earlier biplane, SBU-1.

The other entries in the design competition included the Brewster XSBA-1, the Hall XPTBH-2, the Northrop XBT-1 and the Douglas XTBD-1. The Brewster, Northrop and Douglas designs were all-metal monoplanes, while the Hall design was a twin-engine, twin-float seaplane.

The Navy also ordered prototypes of a number of biplane designs in case the monoplane projects failed to gain acceptance. Great Lakes entered two biplanes, the XB2G-1, an improved version of the BG-1 dive bomber which carried the bomb load internally and had retractable landing gear, and the XTBG-1 torpedo bomber. This ungainly looking aircraft also featured retractable landing gear and carried the torpedo internally. The torpedoman sat in a small compartment located slightly ahead of the leading edge of the top wing. This design could not hope to compete with the Douglas XTBD-1 and did not progress beyond the prototype stage.

Grumman's biplane, the XSBF-1, was developed from the XSF-2 which was basically an SF-1 with a bigger engine. This type was not deemed acceptable by the Navy and was not produced. The Curtiss biplane competitor, the XSBC-3 was accepted for production and an order was placed for eighty-three aircraft on 29 August 1936. So while the monoplane was being developed for service, biplanes continued to be produced and see active service.

In order to back up the XSB2U-1 design, Vought also developed a biplane entry, the XSB3U-1. The prototype XSB3U-1 was converted from the last production SBU-1 and

This large scale model of the XSB2U-1 was used by Vought for wind tunnel testing during November of 1934. (Vought via J. H. Weathers, Jr.)

Competitors

Brewster XSBA-1

Northrup XBT-1

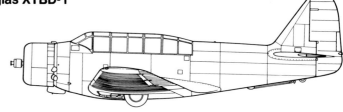

Douglas XTBD-1

Vought XSB3U-1

except for the prototype's unique system of landing gear retraction, the aircraft failed to impress the Navy. The retractable landing gear on the XSB3U-1 retracted backward into the fuselage lower center section and was covered by fairings which were bolted to the landing gear struts. This form of retractable landing gear stowage was far more streamlined than the Curtiss and Grumman designs of the time.

Of the monoplane competitors, all but the Hall XPTBH-1 were accepted for fleet service by the Navy. The Douglas XTBD-1 was accepted and they received a contract for 114 aircraft under the designtion TBD-1 on 3 February 1936. The Brewster XSBA-1, the only mid-wing monoplane submitted, went into production as the SBN-1 at the Naval Aircraft Factory. The Northrop XBT-1 had been entered in the competition as a combination dive bomber/scout aircraft and BuAer decided to develop the design as a dive bomber. Eventually it developed into the most widely used dive bomber of the Second World War, the Douglas SBD Dauntless.

While the U.S. Navy was changing over from the biplane to the monoplane, these same developments were also taking place in a number of other countries. In Germany, the Junkers-Flugzeugwerke had begun work on a prototype dive bomber that would evolve into the famous Ju-87 series used by the Luftwaffe throughout the Second World War. Japan was also working on a dive bomber prototype that would later see action over Hawaii on 7 December 1941. The Aichi D3A, code-named Val, was responsible for a great deal of the damage inflicted on the U.S. fleet at Pearl Harbor that disastrous Sunday morning. Among the casualties were a number of SB2Us of VMSB-231 at Marine Corps Air Station, Ewa.

The XSB2U-1 prototype emerged as a single engine, two seat, low wing, cantilever, retractable landing gear monoplane which retained the metal and fabric covered fuselage like the earlier SBU-1. Additionally, most of the tail and wing surfaces were also fabric covered, the wing being almost completely fabric except for a metal leading edge. The wing had a hydraulically operated trailing edge flap installed on the lower wing center section. Additionally, to assist in slowing the aircraft for carrier landings, the ailerons could be dropped to act as auxiliary flaps. The prototype was powered by a 700 hp Pratt and Whitney R-1535-78 fourteen cylinder air cooled radial engine driving a two blade Hamilton Standard constant speed propeller.

The XSB2U-1 on the company ramp after a test flight on 1 May 1936. The canopy on the early prototype had very few support frames which was found to cause problems and was later modified. (Peter M. Bowers)

The XSB2U-1 prototype was modified with additional canopy framing to strengthen the canopy. The aircraft was overall Aluminum dope with Black codes. The aircraft was lost on 20 August 1936. (Vought via Peter M. Bowers)

The aircraft flew for the first time on 4 January 1936 at Rentchler Field, Hartford, Connecticut. After a series of manufacturer's trials, the aircraft was delivered to the Navy at NAS Anacostia on 2 July 1936. During the Navy tests a number of problems were uncovered. It had been intended to equip the aircraft with a special dive brake propeller; however, this device quickly proved to be difficult to use and technically unsatisfactory. As a replacement system, Vought constructed a dive flap that was to be mounted near the wing leading edge. This flap consisted of a number of finger-like spars that, during normal flight, were flush with the wing surface. On entering a dive they were extended at right angles to the wing surface to slow the aircraft. These flaps failed to work satisfactorily because they caused so much drag that full engine power was needed to maintain control. Additionally, the flaps caused severe aileron buffeting and weighed some 140 pounds. In the event, it was decided to adopt a shallower dive angle and to extend the landing gear to act as a form of brake. The prototype was modified with additional bracing being installed on the pilot's and observer's canopies.

The prototype was lost on 20 August 1936 when, during stall tests at low altitude, it spun in, killing the pilot and observer. The SB2U had a tendency to go into a spin if the aircraft entered a high speed stall. This problem was never corrected and would stay with the SB2U over its entire service life. With experience, however, most Naval Aviators adjusted to the phenomenon and, given enough altitude, it caused no real problem.

Despite the tragic accident, the Navy liked the aircraft well enough to award Vought with a contract worth $2,240,995 for fifty-four production aircraft under the designation SB2U-1 on 26 October 1936.

Development

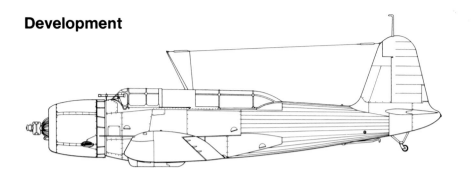

XSB2U-1 (Early)

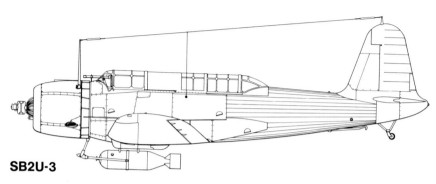

SB2U-3

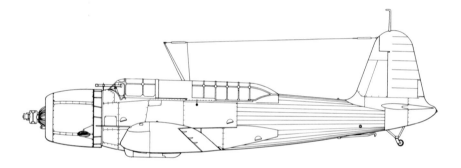

XSB2U-1 (Late)

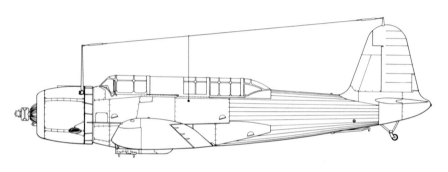

V-156-F

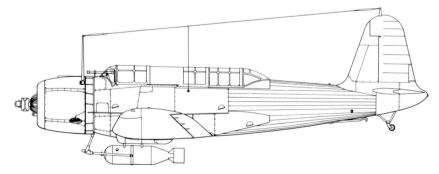

SB2U-1/2

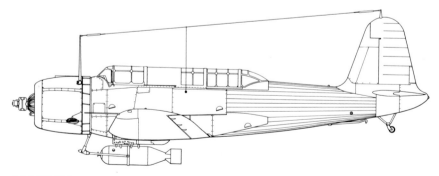

V-156-B1

SB2U-1

The first deliveries of a production SB2U-1 to the fleet took place on 13 December 1937, when Bombing Squadron Three (VB-3) aboard the aircraft carrier USS SARATOGA received their first SB2U-1 (BuNo 0727). The production SB2U-1 differed little from the prototype. The aircraft had the 700 hp Pratt & Whitney engine replaced by a 825 hp Pratt and Whitney R-1535-96 radial and the cowling was changed with a combined oil cooler/carburetor air intake being installed high on the starboard side of the cowling. The exhaust was relocated from the underside of the cowling to a location somewhat higher and to the rear. The radio mast was repositioned from the fuselage spine between the cockpits to a position on the port side of the nose in front of the pilot's cockpit. The canopy framing was also changed, with additional, stronger frames being added to both the pilot's and observer's canopies.

The SB2U-1 was armed with a forward firing Browning .30 caliber machine gun mounted in the starboard wing outside the propeller arc and a second Browning .30 caliber machine gun in the rear cockpit on a flexible ring mount. The offensive bomb load consisted of a single 1,000 pound bomb carried on a fuselage centerline rack or two 500 pound bombs which were carried on racks mounted on the wing center section outboard of the landing gear. The centerline bomb could be replaced with a 50 gallon auxiliary fuel tank to extend the aircraft's range for the scouting role.

During the years prior to World War II, the U.S. Navy used color coded paint schemes that readily identified each aircraft by section and position within each section, while the tail colors identified the squadron's carrier.

The first SB2U-1 delivered to VB-3 was overall Aluminum dope and carried the fuselage code 3-B-1, identifying it as the squadron commander's aircraft. The aircraft's tail surfaces were painted Glossy White to signify the SARATOGA. The aircraft carried a Gloss Red fuselage band and cowl ring, indicating that this aircraft was flown by the leader of Section 1. There was a Gloss Red section stripe painted diagonally across the Gloss Orange-Yellow wing uppersurface and the Black High Hat squadron insignia was carried on the fuselage center section below the cockpit.

The standard Navy eighteen aircraft squadron was divided into six three aircraft sections with each section being assigned a color. Red for Section 1, White for Section 2, True Blue for Section 3, Black for Section 4, Willow Green for Section 5 and Lemon Yellow for Section 6. There were three aircraft in a section and the section leader's aircraft had the entire cowl ring painted in the section color. The second aircraft within the section had the top half of the cowl ring painted and the third aircraft had the bottom half of the cowl ring painted in the section color.

Red - was originally assigned to USS LANGLEY (CV-1) until that ship was converted to a seaplane tender, then it was re-assigned to USS YORKTOWN (CV-5).

White - was used by the USS SARATOGA (CV-3).

True Blue - was assigned to USS ENTERPRISE (CV-6) which was still under construction.

Black - was originally assigned to USS YORKTOWN but later re-assigned to a carrier under construction (USS WASP CV-7).

Production SB2U-1s undergo final preparations before delivery at the Vought factory. The production SB2U-1 featured a prominent air intake on the cowling that supplied air to both the oil cooler and the carburetor. (Vought via J.H. Weathers, Jr.)

Cowling Development

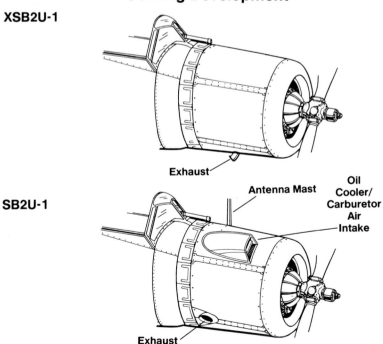

XSB2U-1

Exhaust

SB2U-1

Antenna Mast

Oil Cooler/Carburetor Air Intake

Exhaust

Willow Green - identified aircraft assigned to USS RANGER (CV-4).

Lemon Yellow - was used by the USS LEXINGTON (CV-2).

With the exception of three test aircraft, the entire production run of SB2U-1s was delivered to two squadrons, VB-3 and VB-2. A total of eighteen SB2U-1s were delivered to VB-3 between 13 December 1937 and 1 March 1938. The squadron became the first Navy dive bomber unit to be fully equipped with the new dive bomber and the second Navy squadron to be equipped with a monoplane aircraft (the TBD-1 was the first monoplane to enter Navy service).

The SB2U-1s made their initial appearance aboard USS LEXINGTON on 2 March 1938 when VB-2 received its first aircraft (BuNo 0745). By 26 April 1938, VB-2 had its full complement of twenty-one aircraft. The following month LEXINGTON's Air Group Commander took delivery of a specially painted SB2U-1 (BuNo 0774) to complete the carrier's complement of dive bombers.

Bombing Squadron Three (VB-3) was the first unit to receive the SB2U-1. This SB2U-1 on the ramp at Oakland Airport, California during 1938, was flown by the leader of Section 4, Bombing Squadron 3. 3-B-10 (BuNo 0767) had the fuselage band and engine cowling in Black. (W.T. Larkins via W.L. Swisher)

Pratt & Whitney R-1535-96 Twin Wasp Jr. radial air cooled engines are prepared for installation on production SB2U-1s. Two of the four cowlings have already been painted in section colors. The large opening above the mechanic's head is the combination oil and carburetor cooling air duct. (Vought via J.H. Weathers, Jr.)

SB2U-1s of VB-3 parked on the flight deck of USS SARATOGA (CV-3) on 8 February 1938. The aircraft in the foreground, 3-B-4, was flown by the leader of Section 2, and had White section colors. (National Archives)

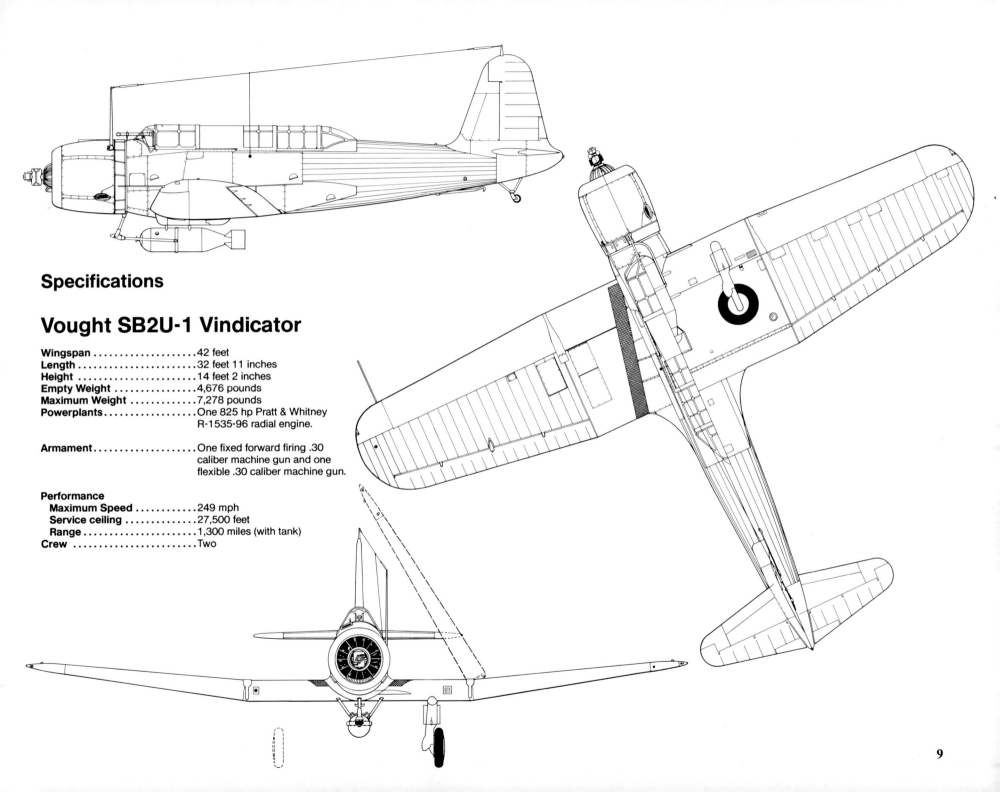

Specifications

Vought SB2U-1 Vindicator

Wingspan .42 feet
Length . . . . .32 feet 11 inches
Height . . . . .14 feet 2 inches
Empty Weight . . . . .4,676 pounds
Maximum Weight . . . . .7,278 pounds
Powerplants . . . . .One 825 hp Pratt & Whitney
R-1535-96 radial engine.

Armament . . . . .One fixed forward firing .30
caliber machine gun and one
flexible .30 caliber machine gun.

Performance
  Maximum Speed . . . . .249 mph
  Service ceiling . . . . .27,500 feet
  Range . . . . .1,300 miles (with tank)
Crew . . . . .Two

The second SB2U-1 of Section 3, 3-B-8, lands aboard USS SARATOGA during 1938. The top half of the cowl ring and wing chevron is True Blue. The aircraft is carrying practice bomb dispensers in place of the outboard wing racks. (Navy)

Equipped with a 50 gallon drop tank on the centerline rack, this SB2U-1 (BuNo 0772), chocked on the ramp of Oakland Airport during 1938 was one of VB-3's spare aircraft and was flown by Aviation Cadet Carter. This aircraft later served with VB-9 in 1942-43. (W.T. Larkins via W.L. Swisher)

An SB2U-1 (BuNo 0757) of VB-2 on the ramp at Bakersfield, California on 14 December 1939. The aircraft was flown by the leader of Section 1 (Insignia Red section color) who was also the squadron commander, LCDR H.D. Felt. (W.L. Swisher)

This SB2U-1 of Scout Bombing Two (VB-2), 2-B-17 (BuNo 0761) carries the squadron insignia on the fuselage side in Black with the knight's plume in the section color. The tail color and top half of the cowling ring is Lemon Yellow, as is the top half of the engine cowling. (CAPT Mark T. Whittier, USN Ret. via J.H. Weathers, Jr.)

This SB2U-1 (BuNo 0773) took part in the aircraft display at the Cleveland Air Races during 1939. The diagonal stripe on the fuselage identified this -1 as the personal aircraft of the Air Group Commander aboard USS RANGER. The stripe was Willow Green outlined in White and the tail color was also Willow Green. (Cernak via J.H. Weathers, Jr)

Wing Mounts

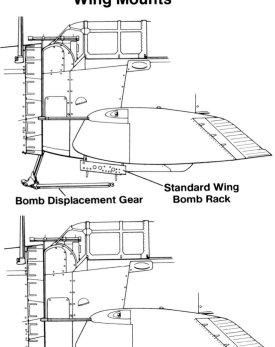

Bomb Displacement Gear

Standard Wing Bomb Rack

Practice Bomb Dispenser

This SB2U-1 (BuNo 0762), 2-B-16, was flown by the leader of Section 6 and had the fuselage band and tail in Lemon Yellow. The aircraft carries a 50 gallon drop tank on the centerline and practice bomb carriers in place of the wing bomb racks. (W.L. Swisher)

SB2U-2

On 27 January 1938, the Navy placed a follow-on contract with Vought for fifty-eight SB2U aircraft. The contract specified some changes in the aircraft's internal equipment resulting in a change in designation from SB2U-1 to SB2U-2. Externally, however, the SB2U-2 was identical to the SB2U-1. The first production SB2U-2 was delivered to NAS Anacostia on 29 August 1938.

Bombing Squadron Four (VB-4), the Black Panthers, became the third squadron to re-equip with the SB2U when they received their first SB2U-2 during December of 1938. While the SB2U-2 differed little from the SB2U-1, it was a completely new and different experience for the Panthers. The squadron had been assigned to the USS RANGER (CV-4) flying the Great Lakes BG-1 biplane and the transition to the SB2U-2 finally brought the Panthers into the "modern" era.

Although there were no external changes specified for the SB2U-2, squadron personnel soon found that outboard wing panels of the two variants were not interchangable (although they should have been). It was found that the lower wing fold hinge assembly on the SB2U-1 would not mate with the SB2U-2 wing.

The first production SB2U-2 (BuNo 1326) on a test flight during late 1938. This aircraft later went into squadron service with Scouting Seventy-two (VS-72) during April of 1941. (Navy via J.M. Elliott)

An SB2U-2 (BuNo 1327) of Fighting 2 at Naval Air Station North Island (San Diego), California during July of 1939. This SB2U was used as a utility aircraft by the Flying Chiefs of VF-2. The tail was Lemon Yellow with Insignia Red stripes and the aircraft carried no section colors. (W.L. Swisher)

The port side of the SB2U-2 pilot's cockpit contained the throttle, mixture controls, propeller controls and landing gear retraction lever. (Navy via J.M. Elliott)

The starboard side of the pilot's cockpit contained the flap controls, electrical distribution panel and oxygen regulator. The object above the upper center of the instrument panel is the telescopic gun sight. (Navy via J.M. Elliott)

The starboard side of the observer/gunner's cockpit of an SB2U-2 (BuNo 1326). The round object is the Direction Finder (DF) loop antenna and next to it is a radio telegraph code transmission key. (Navy via J.M. Elliott)

The port side of the rear cockpit contained the radio trailing antenna reel and its controls, along with other radio equipment. The gunner sat inside the ring gun mount on a fully rotating seat. (Navy via J.M. Elliott)

Bomb Displacement Gear

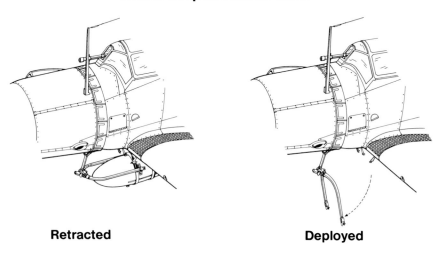

Retracted   **Deployed**

An SB2U-2 (BuNo 1342) of VB-3 at NAS North Island, San Diego, California on 7 August 1939. On 1 July 1939 VB-4 was redesignated VB-3 and assigned to USS SARATOGA. At this time the tail color was being repainted from Willow Green to White and the new squadron designation number, 3, had not been painted on the fuselage. (W.L. Swisher)

This SB2U-2 has a smoke tank installed on the centerline bomb displacement gear. The centerline bomb rack was stressed for loads up to 1,000 pounds. The displacement gear was designed to swing the bomb clear of the propeller arc before releasing it. (Navy via J.M. Elliott)

In Service

Bombing Squadrons Two and Three (VB-2 and VB-3) continued to fly the SB2U-1 with the Pacific Fleet during the years immediately preceding the Second World War II. Both units began to re-equip with the SB2U-2 during 1939-40 on an "as needed" basis as accidents reduced the number of available SB2U-1s. Before long the three fleet SB2U units were operating a mix of both sub-types.

In shipboard service, the SB2U represented a major improvement over existing dive bomber/scout aircraft. Deck crews aboard the carriers had to get used to the manual wing fold system of the SB2U, one of the first aircraft to employ such a system. Pilots had to get used to the higher diving speeds and the lack of responsiveness when compared to the earlier SBC and SBU biplane dive bombers the SB2U replaced.

Besides the dive bomber squadrons, SB2U-1s and SB2U-2s were also assigned to other (non-VB) squadrons during the pre-war period. One of the largest non-VB squadrons to use the SB2U was Scouting Squadron Seventy-Two (VS-72) aboard USS WASP. VS-72 received the first of fourteen SB2U-2s (BuNo 1357) coded 72-S-1, direct from the Vought factory during July of 1939 and deployed aboard USS WASP during April of 1940.

One unusual squadron deployment was with Torpedo Squadron Three (VT-3). VT-3 received six SB2U-2s, operating them for some five months between February and June of 1939. As a torpedo bomber squadron, VT-3 was equipped with the Douglas TBD-1 Devastator and the six SB2U-2s were used to train Naval Aviation Cadets who were assigned to VT-3 for advanced training. These cadets and the SB2Us were later transferred to VS-72. It is not known if the SB2U-2s assigned to VT-3 ever carried VT-3 markings.

One SB2U-2 was delivered to the Aviation Pavilion at the New York World's Fair on 24 April 1939. The aircraft was painted to represent "72-S-4," an aircraft of VS-72, but it never actually served with that squadron. After the fair closed BuNo 1375 was delivered to VB-4 during December of 1940.

At least one SB2U-2 (BuNo 1381) was assigned directly to Fleet Tactical Unit One on 21 June 1939. It was one of three VM (Miscellaneous) aircraft assigned to the Commander, Aircraft Battle Force, Pacific Fleet .

A number of SB2U-1s and SB2U-2s were assigned as utility aircraft for Fighter (VF) Squadrons:

VF-2	BuNo.	Dates Assigned
SB2U-1	0775	July 1938 to December 1938, July 1939 to July 1940
SB2U-1	0726	July 1940 to October 1940
SB2U-2	1327	November 1938 to July 1939
VF-3		
SB2U-1	0775	December 1938 to July 1939
SB2U-2	1327	July 1939 to October 1940
VF-4		
SB2U-1	0745	August 1939 to February 1940

This SB2U-2 (BuNo 1337), 4-B-8, of VB-4 made a wheels up landing at Las Vegas, Nevada on 15 April 1939. The aircraft was flown by ENS C.D. Mott, who later flew as flight leader with the 2nd Pursuit Squadron, American Volunteer Group (AVG) in Rangoon, Burma. He was shot down in early 1942 and survived the war as a POW. (C.D. Mott via J.H. Weathers, Jr.)

One of the "stars" of the Warner Brothers motion picture "Dive Bomber" on the NAS North Island ramp on 28 March 1941. The film had some of the most beautiful flight sequences ever filmed of pre-war Navy aircraft. This same aircraft later served with VF-71 and VS-72 before being retired on 31 December 1942. (Warner Brothers via W.L. Swisher)

A Black tailed SB2U-2 of VS-72 at La Guardia Field, New York during October 1939. This SB2U-2 was one of six delivered to VT-3 between February and June of 1939. Aviation Cadets attached to VT-3 trained with the aircraft, then flew them back to the east coast where they became part of VS-72. This SB2U-2 (BuNo 1362) was lost at sea on 27 March 1942. (Warren Shipp via W.L. Swisher)

The Aviation Pavilion at the 1939 World's Fair in New York had a number of Navy aircraft on display including (from right) a Curtiss SBC, North American BC-1A and Vought SB2U. The last suspended aircraft was an Army Air Corps YA-19 prototype. (National Archives)

An SB2U-2 (BuNo 1375) was suspended from the overhead in the Aviation Pavilion at the 1939 New York World's Fair. While painted to represent an aircraft assigned to VS-72, this SB2U never actually served with that squadron. (Navy via J.H. Weathers, Jr.)

VF-7		
SB2U-2	1356	September 1939 to December 1940

VF-71		
SB2U-2	1333	May 1941 to June 1941

VF-72		
SB2U-2	1356	September 1939 to December 1940
SB2U-2	1336	April 1941 to June 1941
SB2U-2	1333	August 1941 to November 1941

Several SB2Us were assigned as personal aircraft for five of the six Air Group Commanders within the Fleet:

	BuNo.	Assigned

LEXINGTON		
SB2U-1	0774	June 1938 to January 1940
SB2U-2	1349	February 1940 to August 1940

SARATOGA		
SB2U-2	1328	November 1938 to unknown

Five SB2U-2s (including BuNos 1372, 1369, 1364) parked on the flight line at Naval Air Station Norfolk, Virginia during 1941. The large U.S. insignia on the cowling identified these aircraft as being assigned to Neutrality Patrol duty. (CAPT L.E. Dailey via Harry Gann)

RANGER		
SB2U-1	0773	July 1939 to June 1940

YORKTOWN		
SB2U-1	0763	June 1941 to October 1941
SB2U-2	1354	September 1939 to June 1941

WASP		
SB2U-2	1379	July 1939 to July 1941

SB2U-2s of VS-72 were active participants in the Neutrality Patrol and carried the star insignia specified on 19 March 1940. VS-72 was the largest non-dive bomber unit to fly the SB2U. (CAPT L.E. Dailey via Harry Gann)

The directive that specified the use of the Neutrality Patrol star was AER-E-255-HY, QW-19, F-39-1, Technical Note 6-40. This directive stated that SB2U aircraft participating in patrol activities would carry a two foot diameter star insignia on the engine cowling. The star was to be centered two feet aft of the forward edge of the cowl panel (part number CV-42859) and fourteen inches below the upper edge of the cowl side panel. (CAPT L.E. Dailey via Harry Gann)

Marine Fighter Squadron One (VMF-1) flew a single SB2U-1 (BuNo 0769) as a utility aircraft between 1938 and 1939.

During January of 1939, the SARATOGA was ordered to the Bremerton, Washington Navy Yard for overhaul and did not accompany the Battle Fleet on the annual cruise to Panama and the Caribbean that took place between January and May. While the ship was in the yards, the SARATOGA Air Group remained at NAS North Island, San Diego, California.

A decision was made to substitute two SARATOGA Air Group squadrons, VF-3 (F3F-1s) and VS-3 (SBC-3s) on the LEXINGTON in place of the ships' regular squadrons, VF-2 (F2F-1s) and VS-2 (SBU-1s). The two LEXINGTON squadrons remained behind at North Island during the cruise period with the rest of the SARATOGA Air Group. Another SARATOGA squadron, VB-3 (SB2U-1s) went aboard RANGER for this cruise in place of VB-4 (SB2U-2s), which remained behind at NAS North Island.

At the end of the 1939 Caribbean Cruise, while RANGER was still in the Atlantic, a decision was made to permanently assign RANGER to the Atlantic Fleet because of the developing threat of war in Europe. As a result, CNO issued a directive, effective 1 July 1939, that redesignated VB-3 as VB-4 with permanent assignment to the RANGER Air

VS-72's squadron insignia was known as the *Centaur Vampire*. The Bat and land masses on the globe were Blue-Gray, the globe was Yellow and the Centaur's face was pink. The aircraft also carried a White Battle E award. (CAPT L.E. Dailey via Harry Gann)

Group. At this same time VB-4 was redesignated as VB-3 with permanent assignment to the SARATOGA Air Group.

Neutrality Patrols

Shortly after the start of the Second World War in Europe, the U.S. Atlantic Squadron was ordered to establish surface and air patrols in the Atlantic Ocean covering eight specific areas. This action was known as the Neutrality Patrol and aircraft from WASP, YORKTOWN and RANGER played an important part in these predominantly anti-submarine patrols. Aircraft involved in the patrols carried a U.S. national insignia on the fuselage, and the directive covering the SB2U, issued on 19 March 1940, stated that "...a two foot diameter star insignia would be carried on the engine cowling...."

The eight patrol areas were:

PATROL 0: Placentia Bay and Halifax, south to 40 ° N.

PATROL 1: Ran along a northwest-southeast line off Georges Shoal.

PATROL 2: Consisted of a triangle from Newport to 43° 05'N/65° 30'W to 37° 50' N/70 ° 20' W.

PATROL 3: Covered the waters between Chesapeake Lightship at 37° 50' N/70 ° 20'W to 34° 10' N/73° 05' W.

This SB2U-1 was delivered to the Marine Corps on 4 May 1938 and served with Marine Fighter Squadron One (VMF-1) at MCAS Quantico, Virginia. It was later transferred to VS-72 then to VS-42 and ended its career at NAS Glenview, Illinois, in a Carrier Qualification Training Unit. It was finally retired on 31 April 1943.(USMC via W.F. Gemeinhardt)

This SB2U-1 (0773) was assigned to the Commander of the air group aboard USS RANGER and carries a Commander Air Group (CAG) band on the fuselage. The stripe and tail were Willow Green and the stripe had a thin White outline. (James C. Fahey via Harry Gann)

PATROL 9: Covered the coast between Newport and Cape Hatteras out to a distance of 300 miles.

PATROL 6: Included the Florida Straits, Yucatan Channel and adjacent waters.

PATROLS 7 and 8: Operated at the Commander Caribbean Sea Frontier's discretion in the Eastern Caribbean south of 23° 10' N.

WASP and her squadrons were the first to undertake a Neutrality Patrol, deploying on 26 April 1941. RANGER began her patrol on 9 May and at the completion of her first patrol on 23 May, the SB2U-2s of VS-41 and the F4F-3s of VF-41 were shifted to YORKTOWN which was about the commence her first patrol. On 31 May 1941, YORK-TOWN got underway. The displaced YORKTOWN squadrons (VF-5, VS-5 and VB-5) went aboard RANGER and made one patrol before being returned to the United States for equipment updating.

The Marine Corps insignia was carried on the fuselage side under the cockpit. All Navy SB2U-1s were delivered in full unit markings while the Marine aircraft were not. (USMC via W.F. Gemeinhardt)

This SB2U-1 was assigned to VMF-1 and served as a utility aircraft, target tug and squadron hack. The stripes on the rudder are Insignia Blue (trailing edge) Insignia White and Insignia Red. All lettering was in Black. (LeRoy McCallum via W.F. Gemeinhardt)

A Marine SB2U, 1-MF-19, at Bourne Field, Charlotte Amalie, St. Thomas, Virgin Islands during 1938. The Marines were stationed here during maneuvers. The wing uppersurface was painted Gloss Orange-Yellow. (LeRoy McCallum via W. F. Gemeinhardt)

SB2U-3

The SB2U-3 was developed to fill a Marine Corps requirement for a dive bomber with a longer range than the BG-1s then in service. To meet this requirement for long-range capability Vought offered the Marine Corps a new variant of the SB2U with increased fuel capacity. The proposal was accepted and on 25 September 1939 Vought received a contract for fifty-seven aircraft under the designation SB2U-3.

The XSB2U-3 prototype started out as a standard production SB2U-1 and was converted to the proposed SB2U-3 configuration. The changes included an increase in the span of the horizontal stabilizers from 13 feet 4 inches to 15 feet 2 1/16 inches, a substantially increased internal fuel supply, provision for four forward firing .50 caliber machine guns (normally only one was fitted) and replacing the gunner's .30 caliber machine gun with a .50 caliber weapon. The engine was changed from the 825 hp Pratt & Whitney R-1535-96 to the 825 hp Pratt & Whitney R-1535-02. These changes resulted in an increase of some 921 pounds in the aircraft's empty weight. The improvements made to the basic airplane did nothing to improve its performance and the increased weight of fuel caused the SB2U-3's performance to suffer.

In addition to increasing the main fuel tank capability, three additional tanks were added to the aircraft center section. These tanks were unprotected and would later prove to be a problem when in combat. The increased tankage plus the 50'gallon external auxiliary centerline tank gave the SB2U-3 a range of 2,640 miles (or a search radius of 1,320 miles). Armed with a 1,000 pound bomb load the SB2U-3 had a combat radius of 560 miles.

The XSB2U-3 was flown for the first time during February of 1939. After a brief period of testing, the aircraft was returned to the Vought factory where it was fitted with a pair of Edo floats. It was returned to NAS Anacostia, Washington, D.C. to resume testing during April. Difficulties in water handling led to the aircraft being modified with a large ventral fin and larger water rudders on the floats. In the event, the Navy decided that there was only limited value in the float scout aircraft and the production contract for the SB2U-3 specified that all fifty-seven aircraft (BuNos 2044 through 2100) would be produced as landplanes with retractable landing gear. It is a little known fact that the first production SB2U-3 was actually delivered as a float aircraft, then reconfigured as a land plane before formal acceptance by the Marines.

It was during the production run of the SB2U-3 that the Navy decided to give the aircraft a name and bestowed the name Vindicator to the entire SB2U series. Deliveries of SB2U-3s began on 14 March 1941 when VMS-2, based at NAS North Island, San Diego, California, received their first aircraft (BuNo 2045). A total of twenty-seven OS2U-3s (BuNos 2045 through 2071) were delivered to VMS-2 between 14 March and 30 April 1940. VMS-2 was followed by VMS-1 at MCAS Quantico, Virginia, on 9 May. Like its sister squadron, VMS-1 received a total of twenty-seven aircraft with the last being delivered during July of 1941.

The first production SB2U-3 (2044) went to NAS Anacostia, Washington, D.C. for testing after it was returned to the land plane configuration. Squadron deliveries began on 14 March 1941 when BuNo 2045 was accepted by VMS-2 at San Diego. The aircraft was later damaged beyond repair on 30 April 1942. (USMC via J.M. Elliott)

Two aircraft (BuNos 2072 and 2100) went to Marine Utility Squadron Two (VMJ-2) and VMJ-151 on 2 May and 22 July 1941 respectively, completing deliveries of SB2U-3s to the Marine Corps.

It was on YORKTOWN's second Neutrality Patrol, beginning on 29 June 1941, that the first Marine Corps SB2U-3 squadron saw duty on the patrol. Marine Scouting Squadron One (VMS-1) based at Quantico, deployed aboard YORKTOWN for the cruise. In addition to Neutrality Patrols, Marine OS2U-3s were deployed to Reykjavik, Iceland on 7 July 1941. The preparations for war with Germany took another step forward with the establishment of this garrison and the beginnings of air operations by both Army Air Corps and Navy/Marine units out of Iceland.

The XSB2U-3 prototype (BuNo 0779) was used on both wheel and floats. In the event the Navy decided that there was no need for a float scout aircraft and the SB2U-3 contract specified that all aircraft would be delivered as land planes. (Peter M. Bowers)

The XSB2U-3 prototype undergoes water handling tests during April of 1939. The aircraft proved to be unstable in the water and was modified with larger water rudders to increase directional stability. (Peter M. Bowers)

XSB2U-3 Float Installation

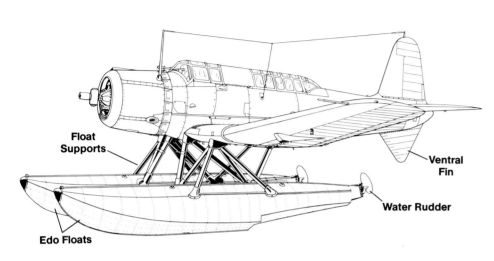

Float Supports

Edo Floats

Ventral Fin

Water Rudder

The last production SB2U-1 was converted to the XSB2U-3 configuration and tested as a float plane. The floats proved unsatisfactory for Marine Corps use and the project was abandoned. The large ventral stabilizing fin was fitted after the aircraft was found to be directionally unstable. (Navy via Peter M. Bowers)

The first production SB2U-3 was actually completed as a float plane, and was reconfigured to a land plane after the Navy cancelled the float scout aircraft project. The aircraft was officially accepted by the Marines after it was reconfigured. (Peter M. Bower)

23

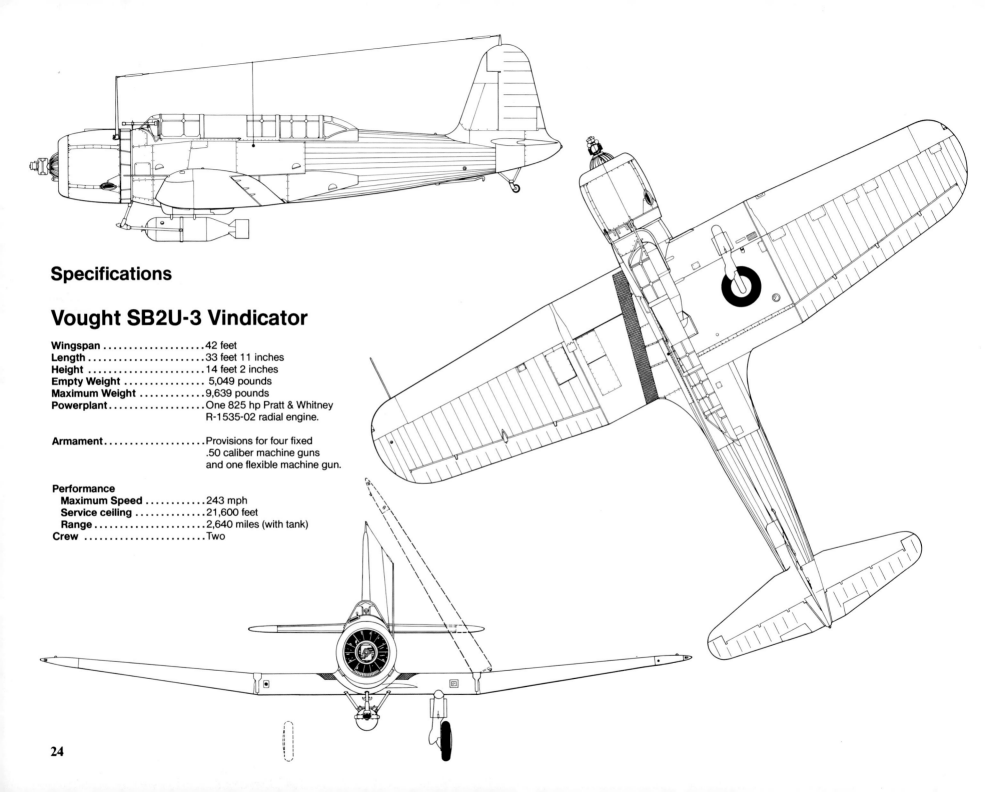

Specifications

Vought SB2U-3 Vindicator

Wingspan .42 feet
Length . . . . .33 feet 11 inches
Height . . . . .14 feet 2 inches
Empty Weight . . . . 5,049 pounds
Maximum Weight . . . . .9,639 pounds
Powerplant . . . . .One 825 hp Pratt & Whitney
                                        R-1535-02 radial engine.

Armament . . . . .Provisions for four fixed
                                        .50 caliber machine guns
                                        and one flexible machine gun.

Performance
  Maximum Speed . . . . .243 mph
  Service ceiling . . . . .21,600 feet
  Range .2,640 miles (with tank)
Crew . . . . .Two

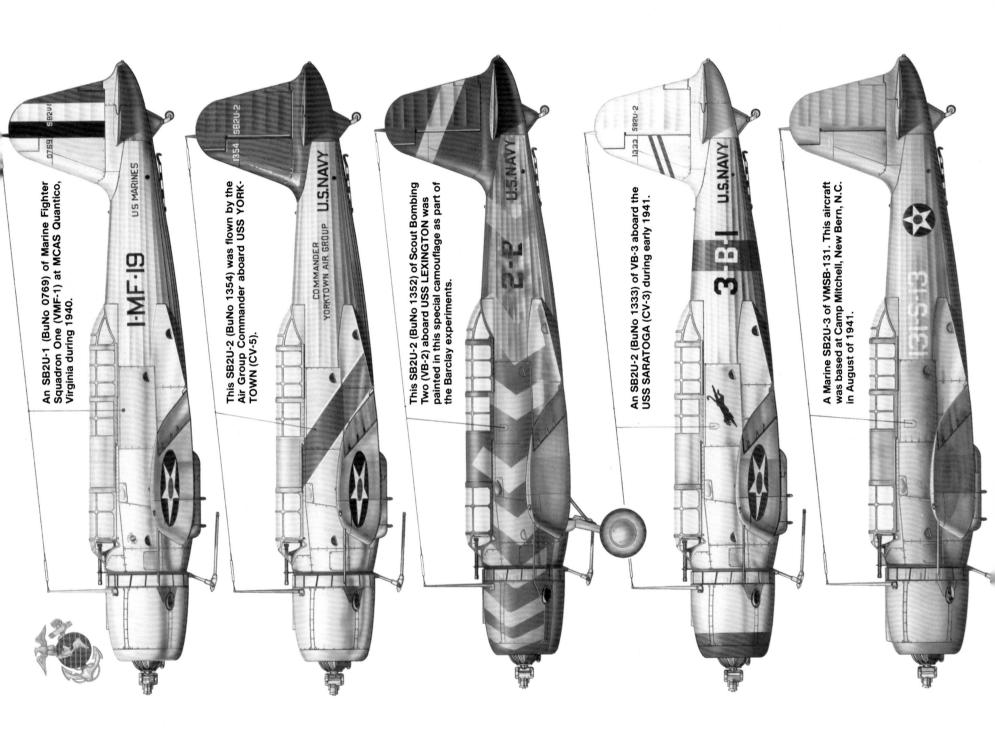

An SB2U-1 (BuNo 0769) of Marine Fighter Squadron One (VMF-1) at MCAS Quantico, Virginia during 1940.

This SB2U-2 (BuNo 1354) was flown by the Air Group Commander aboard USS YORK-TOWN (CV-5).

This SB2U-2 (BuNo 1352) of Scout Bombing Two (VB-2) aboard USS LEXINGTON was painted in this special camouflage as part of the Barclay experiments.

An SB2U-2 (BuNo 1333) of VB-3 aboard the USS SARATOGA (CV-3) during early 1941.

A Marine SB2U-3 of VMSB-131. This aircraft was based at Camp Mitchell, New Bern, N.C. in August of 1941.

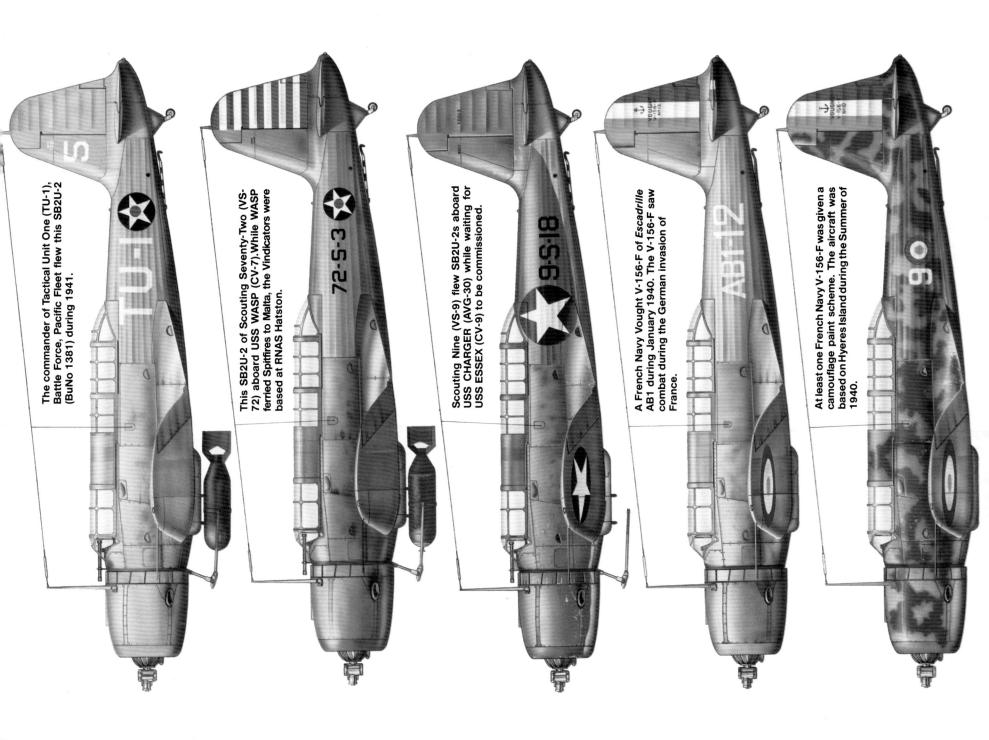

The commander of Tactical Unit One (TU-1), Battle Force, Pacific Fleet flew this SB2U-2 (BuNo 1381) during 1941.

This SB2U-2 of Scouting Seventy-Two (VS-72) aboard USS WASP (CV-7). While WASP ferried Spitfires to Malta, the Vindicators were based at RNAS Hatston.

Scouting Nine (VS-9) flew SB2U-2s aboard USS CHARGER (AVG-30) while waiting for USS ESSEX (CV-9) to be commissioned.

A French Navy Vought V-156-F of *Escadrille* AB1 during January 1940. The V-156-F saw combat during the German invasion of France.

At least one French Navy V-156-F was given a camouflage paint scheme. The aircraft was based on Hyeres Island during the Summer of 1940.

SB2U-3s of Marine Scout Bombing Squadron One Thirty-One (VMSB-131) share the grass strip at Camp Mitchell, New Bern, North Carolina on 15 August 1941 with a Curtiss SBC-4 Helldiver of the First Marine Air Wing. (J.R. Cram via J.H. Weathers, Jr.)

Horizontal Stabilizer Development

SB2U-1/2

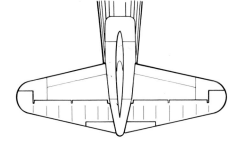

SB2U-3

Lengthened Stabilizer

An SB2U-3, 1-S-16, of VMS-1 in flight during 1941. The aircraft was camouflaged in overall Non-specular Light Gray and carried a U.S. star on the fuselage. All lettering was in White. (Vought via B. R. Jackson)

The pilot of this Marine SB2U-3 was 2LT James H. Marmande. Marmande was later lost while flying an SB2U-3 Vindicator of VMSB-241 on 4 June 1942 during the Battle of Midway. He and his gunner, PFC Edby Colvin disappeared while on the return flight to Midway Island after attacking the Japanese fleet. (Rudy Arnold via J.M. Elliott)

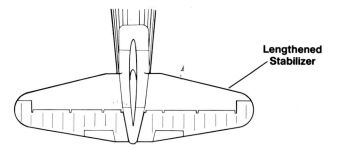

An overall Light Gray SB2U-3, 131-S-13, of VMSB-131 parked on the grass at Camp Mitchell, New Bern, North Carolina during August of 1941. The Marines were taking part in one of a series of war games that were held during 1941. (J.R. Cram via J.H. Weathers, Jr)

CAPT Jack R. Cram (left) and his rear seat gunner stand beside their SB2U-3 at Camp Mitchell, New Bern, North Carolina on 15 August 1941. On 15 October 1942, Cram flew a daring PBY torpedo mission against a Japanese invasion force off Guadalcanal. His PBY-5A, the Blue Goose, was hit by some 1,975 machine gun bullets and for this action, MAJ Cram was awarded the Navy Cross. (J.R. Cram via J.H. Weathers, Jr)

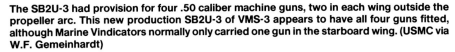

The SB2U-3 had provision for four .50 caliber machine guns, two in each wing outside the propeller arc. This new production SB2U-3 of VMS-3 appears to have all four guns fitted, although Marine Vindicators normally only carried one gun in the starboard wing. (USMC via W.F. Gemeinhardt)

An overall Light Gray SB2U-3, 2-S-16, of VMS-2 on the ramp at MCAS Ewa, Hawaii in 1941. Most of the squadron's aircraft were later destroyed on the ground during the Japanese attack. (A.J. Bibee via the author)

This new production SB2U-3 (BuNo 2050) was delivered to VMS-2 on 14 March 1941. The aircraft was later destroyed on the ground when the Japanese attacked Ewa Marine Corps Air Station, Ewa, Hawaii on 7 December 1941. (USMC via W.F. Gemeinhardt)

An SB2U-3 Vindicator, 231-S-17, of VMSB-231 on its back after flipping over on landing at MCAS/NAS Kaneohe Bay, Hawaii on 11 September 1941. The rear seater at the time was 1LT Richard E. Fleming, USMC. On 5 June 1942, Fleming (then CAPT) was killed flying an SB2U-3 of VMSB-241 on a mission against the Japanese cruiser, MIKUMA. For this action he was awarded the Medal of Honor. (USMC via J.H. Weathers, Jr.)

SB2U-3s, Douglas SBDs and Grumman F3F fighters of Marine Air Group 21 (MAG-21) share the ramp at their base at MCAS Ewa, Hawaii during 1941. This area was heavily bombed during the Japanese attack on 7 December. (USMC via Clay Jansson)

29

V-156-F

During early 1939, Chance-Vought joined with Sikorsky Aircraft and moved its aircraft production to Stratford, Connecticut. The merger of the two companies made it possible for each to concentrate on the development and manufacture of widely differing types of aircraft. Vought concentrated on combat aircraft while Sikorsky continued its research and development efforts on helicopters for both military and commercial use.

The threat of war in Europe led the Vought division to outfit an extra SB2U-2 airframe as a company demonstrator to seek export sales for the SB2U series in Europe. The aircraft was sent to Paris for the *Salon de l'Aeronautique* during October of 1938 where it was demonstrated for French officials. This demonstration led the French government, on 22 February 1939, to place a contract for twenty aircraft under the company designation V-156-F.

The Chance Vought V-156 company demonstrator was displayed at the *Salon de l'Aeronautique* during November of 1938. The V-156 demonstrator was later returned to the states and re-engined with a Pratt & Whitney R-1830 Twin Wasp and redesignated the V-167. The Navy was not interested in this variant and Vought retained the aircraft, using it for various tests until it was dropped from the civil register in late 1947. (Lyman A. Bullard, Jr. via J.H. Weathers, Jr.)

While based on the earlier SB2U-2, the V-156-F featured a number of changes particular to the needs of the French Navy. The throttle was reversed so that it operated in the opposite way from U.S. standards (full power in the rearmost position), metric instrumentation replaced U.S. instruments, French radio equipment was installed in place of American radios and French Darne 7.5 MM machine guns replaced the U.S. .30 caliber machine guns. The French were not allowed to use the Vought bomb displacement gear (for security reasons) and it was deleted with the understanding that French Alkan equipment was to be installed after the aircraft were delivered. In the event, by May of 1940, this equipment had still not been installed and most French V-156-F combat missions were carried out using only the underwing bomb racks. The wing mounted fence type dive brakes, rejected by the U.S. Navy, were installed on the V-156-F.

During May of 1939, another order for twenty additional V-156-Fs was received by the Vought company and in June the first V-156-F rolled off the Vought assembly line. The first V-156-Fs arrived at LeHavre during July. They were off-loaded and transported to Orly Field in Paris for assembly and checkout. The first flight took place on 6 August and by the time hostilities began with Germany on 3 September there were thirty-four V-156-Fs in the inventory. Once the war broke out, the remaining V-156-Fs purchased by the French were shipped via Canada to avoid being embargoed under the U.S. Neutrality Act.

Escadrille AB 1 was the first French unit to re-equip with the V-156-F. When the carrier BEARN was declared obsolete for war service, her units were moved ashore. The *Flotille* was split into two parts: the 1st *Flotille de Chasse* (F1C), equipped with fighters and the 1st *Flotille d'Attaque* (F1A) consisting of AB 1 and AB 3, both flying the V-156-F. These units flew alongside AB 2 and AB 4, equipped with the Loire-Nieuport LN 401/411 dive bomber.

The V-156 prepares for a demonstration flight during January of 1939 at Orly Field, Paris, France. As a result of these demonstrations, the French government purchased forty V-156-F bombers, operating them against the Germans and Italians during the early days of WW II. (Lyman A. Bullard, Jr. via J.H. Weathers, Jr.)

After AB 1 received its full complement of eleven V-156-Fs it was deployed to Lanveoc-Poulmic to complete transition training. Once reaching operational status, AB 1 was moved to Alprecht, near Boulogne, on the Channel coast. From there, during November 1939, the squadron performed maritime patrols and flew protection for Allied convoys operating in the English Channel and the North Sea. The second French unit, AB 3, was formed at Querqueville (Cherbourg) on 1 December 1939.

The V-156-F received its "baptism of fire" on 20 May 1940 when AB 1 took on the task of bombing a number of vital bridges that crossed a canal near Origny-Ste-Benoite on the Oise River. This attack was ordered in an attempt to slow German armored units, even through the Navy pilots had no training or experience in attacking land targets. During this attack, the squadron was caught by a flight of Messerscmitt Bf-109Es and lost five aircraft.

The surviving V-156-Fs of AB 1 participated in covering the Dunkirk evacuation that enabled some 338,226 British and Allied soldiers to reach the safety of England. From 26 May to 4 June, AB 1 attacked German armor and artillery with their remaining six V-156-Fs,

for a loss of one aircraft. By the time France fell, the V-156-F had proven it could carry the fight to the enemy. While not a world class dive bomber, it managed to get through mainly on the wits and courage of the men in the cockpit.

AB 3 was based at Cuers in the south of France and was attacking Italian targets during the waning days of the French war against the Axis. Several targets in Northern Italy were hit by AB 3 on 14 June 1940 when the squadron took off in two groups looking for targets of opportunity. The first group, aircraft numbers 1, 7, 9 and 5 left Cuers at 0345. The second group, 2, 4, 8 and 10 left Cuers one hour later at 0445. The first section, headed by L.V. Pierret with Radio Second Maitre Bour in the rear seat, sighted an Italian submarine on the surface some twenty miles off Albenga. Four V-156-Fs of AB 3 made a perfect bomb run on the ship and scored two hits, sinking the submarine.

The next day six V-156-Fs were lost when their base was attacked by Fiat CR-42 biplane fighters of the *Regia Aeronautica*. On 17 June the surviving aircraft attacked Porto San Stefano Liguria. This was their last operational mission. After this mission the squadron evacuated to Corsica and by 30 August 1940, the V-156-Fs were history.

Armed with a 150 kg (330 pound) underwing bomb, this V-156-F, aircraft number 3, on the ramp at Lanveor-Roulmie was believed to have been assigned to AB 1. The V-156-F did not have the centerline bomb displacement gear installed. (MUSEE de l' AIR via Geoffrey Bussy)

French Navy V-156-Fs operated primarily from land bases during their short service careers. The V-156-F did not have the telescopic sight used by the U.S. Navy SB2U series. (MUSEE de l' AIR via Geoffrey Bussy)

SB2U-2

V-156-F

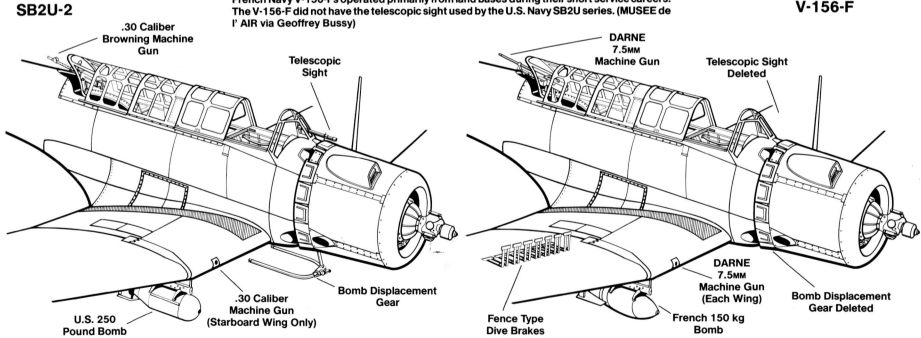

.30 Caliber Browning Machine Gun

Telescopic Sight

U.S. 250 Pound Bomb

.30 Caliber Machine Gun (Starboard Wing Only)

Bomb Displacement Gear

DARNE 7.5MM Machine Gun

Telescopic Sight Deleted

Fence Type Dive Brakes

DARNE 7.5MM Machine Gun (Each Wing)

French 150 kg Bomb

Bomb Displacement Gear Deleted

French navy crewmen board their V-156-F of AB 1 during late 1939. The fence type dive brakes are visible on the port wing uppersurface just outboard of the wing fold line. The squadron and aircraft numbers are in White. (MUSEE de l' AIR via Geoffrey Bussy)

Two V-156-Fs of *Escadrille* AB 1 at Alprecht airfield during the Winter of 1939-40. The V-156-F was painted Semi-gloss Medium Gray overall with (from front) Blue, White and Red rudder stripes. The elevators also carried Blue, White and Red horizontal stripes and the French roundel was carried on the top and bottom of each wing. (MUSEE de l' AIR via Geoffrey Bussy)

Ground crewmen load a 150 kg (330 pound) bomb on the wing rack of a V-156-F of AB 1. The opening in the wing leading edge is the blast port for a Darne 7.5MM machine gun. (SHAA via Geoffrey Bussy)

A French Navy pilot poses next to his V-156-F of AB 1. The aircraft carries two 150 kg bombs on the underwing racks. The V-156-Fs were active in bombing raids against German armor and a number were lost to German fighters. (SHAA via Geoffrey Bussy)

V-156-F of AB 1 on their home field during 1940. The V-156-F flew its last operational mission with the French Navy on 17 June 1940 when three V-156-Fs of AB 3 attacked Porto San Stefano. (SHAA via Geoffrey Bussy)

It is believed that only one V-156-F was painted in a mottle camouflage. This V-156-F, aircraft number 10 of AB3, was at Hyeres Island after the Armistice with the overall Gray mottled with Green and Brown patches. The side number "9" was in White and the upper wing carried large diameter national insignia. (SHAA via Geoffrey Bussy)

Chesapeake

On 28 March 1940 the French government placed an order for an additional fifty V-156-Fs, with deliveries to begin during early 1941. Due to the production of the SB2U-3 for the Marine Corps, it became necessary for Vought to sub-contract many of the V-156-F sub-assemblies. In the event the second production batch of V-156-Fs were not ready for delivery before France fell and the contract was taken over by the British, with the V-156-Fs being redesignated as the V-156-B1.

To meet British requirements a number of changes were made to the V-156-B1. The throttle arrangement was returned to the original design (forward to increase power), the Vought bomb displacement gear was reinstalled, the larger fuel tanks of the SB2U-3 were incorporated, armor protection for the crew and fuel tanks was provided, the forward firing armament was increased to four wing mounted .30 caliber machine guns instead of the single gun used on the SB2U-2 and the fence type wing dive brakes were deleted. Installation of a British type tail hook was considered but this is not known to have actually occurred. It is believed all V-156-B1s retained the U.S. Navy type tail hook.

The aircraft was given the name Chesapeake in British service and were assigned the serial numbers AL908 to AL957. The first Chesapeake flew on 26 February 1941 and by the end of March, the V-156-B1 had been accepted by the British. In spite of the aircraft's overall poor performance in areas vital to carrier operations, some British officials considered using the aircraft as a defensive weapon for seaborne operations from escort carriers. Tests soon revealed that the added weight of fuel, armor and armament made the takeoff run (some 1,700 feet) far too long for carrier operations from British aircraft carriers. Despite this, shipments of the new aircraft to England began during the Summer of 1941.

The first aircraft to arrive at Liverpool were trucked to the nearby aircraft repair depot at Burtonwood. After re-assembly and testing, the aircraft were assigned to various Fleet Air Arm squadrons. The first unit to receive the Chesapeake was No 778 Squadron which conducted tests with the aircraft during June of 1941. The unit was stationed at RNAS Arbroath and operated as a Service Trials Unit, having one or two aircraft on strength for a short period. By December, the squadron had none in their inventory.

During June, No 786 Squadron, a Torpedo Bomber/Reconnaissance Training Squadron based at Crail, received a few Chesapeakes. The unit was to retain the Vought dive bomber for some two years. No 787 Squadron also received a few V-156-B1s for test and evaluation during July.

The only squadron to receive enough Chesapeakes for operational service was No 811 Squadron based at RNAS Lee-on-Solent. The squadron received a total of fourteen aircraft during July of 1941. The aircraft remained on strength for only five months being replaced by Fairey Swordfish aircraft during November.

As the war progressed, No 771 Squadron at Twatt, No 770 Squadron at Crail, No 772 Squadron at Machrihanish and No 776 Squadron at Speke all used a number of Chesapeakes for target-towing duties. During June of 1942, No 784 Squadron was formed and this unit used a few V-156-B1s for night-fighter training. The aircraft were based at Lee-on-Solent until October of 1942, then moved on to Drem. By August of 1943 the squadron had retired all of the V-156-B1s. By May of 1944, the last Chesapeake was withdrawn from Fleet Air Arm (FAA) service when No 770 Squadron retired their last target tug.

A Royal Navy V-156-B1 Chesapeake undergoes a pre-delivery test flight over the Atlantic. V-156-B1s were originally painted overall Sea Gray but later received a Dark Green and Dark Earth uppersufrace camouflage over Sky Blue undersurfaces. (United Technologies Archive)

This was the seventeenth V-156-B1 (AL924) off the production line. It was assigned to No 811 Squadron based at Lee-on-Solent during 1941. The aircraft was camouflaged with Dark Green and Dark Earth uppersurfaces over Sky Blue undersurfaces. (Geoffrey Bussy Collection)

Atlantic Operations

The Atlantic based fleet carriers USS RANGER (CV-4), USS WASP (CV-7) and USS YORKTOWN (CV-5) were all engaged in either normal training missions or anti-submarine operations when the Japanese struck Pearl Harbor on 7 December 1941. When they received word of the Pearl Harbor attack, USS YORKTOWN was in port at the Naval Operating Base (NOB), Norfolk, Virginia, USS RANGER was cruising toward the Cape of Good Hope and USS WASP was anchored in Grassy Bay off the coast of Bermuda.

At the time of the Pearl Harbor attack, RANGER had two Vindicator squadrons: Scouting Forty-one (VS-41) equipped with fourteen SB2U-1s and two SB2U-2s and Scouting Forty-two (VS-42) with twelve SB2U-1s and four SB2U-2s. WASP had Scouting Seventy-one (VS-71) embarked with seven SB2U-1s and ten SB2U-2s (VS-71 also had

three TBD-1s). A second Vindicator sqaudron, Scouting Seventy-two (VS-72) with sixteen SB2U-2s, was also aboard. YORKTOWN carried no Vindicators, since VB-3 had re-equipped with the Douglas SBD-3 Dauntless.

Immediately after the Pearl Harbor attack, YORKTOWN was ordered to the Pacific, arriving at Pearl Harbor during January of 1942. During April of 1942, USS WASP joined with Force W and headed for Gibraltar with a deckload of RAF Spitfire fighters for the British outpost at Malta in the Mediterranean. Just prior to joining the Royal Navy task force, her SB2Us (along with the rest of her air group) were off loaded at Hatston Royal Navy Air Station. In the event, the Vindicator was not to see action with the WASP while the ship operated in the Atlantic.

USS RANGER had been deemed too small for Pacific operations and remained in the Atlantic for most of the war. She operated her SB2U squadrons on convoy escort and anti-submarine missions until the Summer of 1942. When RANGER went into combat off North Africa in November of 1942 as part of Operation TORCH, all the Vindicators were gone, having been replaced by the SBD Dauntless.

Vindicators from VS-42 and VS-41 prepare for launch from USS RANGER (CV-4) on 10 November 1941. At this time, all Navy and Marine Corps aircraft were camouflaged with Non-specular Blue Gray uppersurfaces over Non-specular Light Gray undersurfaces with White lettering. (Navy via J.H. Weathers, Jr.)

A trio of SB2U-2s covered with rime ice during North Atlantic operations in early 1942. The Red and White horizontal tail stripes were ordered in a two page directive, AER-E-2571-BP, F39-5, VV, FF12, 001085 issued on 5 January 1942. They would remain in use for only a short period of time. (National Archives)

An SB2U-2 Vindicator of VS-41 High Hats makes a deck run takeoff from USS RANGER in late 1941. RANGER remained in the Atlantic throughout most of the war and operated the SB2U longer than the other fleet carriers. (National Archives)

SB2U-2s of VS-72 share the flight deck with F4F-3 Wildcat fighters of VF-72 in early 1942. All the aircraft are securely chocked and tied down to prevent movement during rough seas. (National Archives)

VS-72 SB2U-2s are prepared for flight at Royal Navy Air Station Hatston during April 1942. The aircraft are camouflaged Non-specular Blue Gray over Non-specular Light Gray with the undersides of the outer wing panels being painted in the uppersurface color to blend with the rest of the aircraft when folded. (via J.H. Weathers, Jr.)

USS WASP (CV-7) underway during early 1942 with three VS-72 SB2U-2 Vindicators parked on the flight deck. The WASP was lost to enemy action on 15 September 1942. (National Archives)

A section of SB2U-2s of VS-41 High Hats conducts a long range patrol mission off USS RANGER in the Atlantic. The Vindicator did not see combat in the Atlantic, being phased out before Operation TORCH. (Navy via J.M. Elliott)

Eight SB2U-2s of VS-41 conduct maneuvers during late 1942. VS-41 operated off the USS RANGER in the Atlantic during the early part of the war. The Vindicators were replaced by SBDs before the RANGER went into combat off North Africa. (Navy via J.H. Weathers, Jr.)

Vindicator Weapons

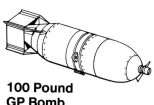

100 Pound GP Bomb

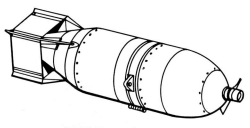

500 Pound GP Bomb

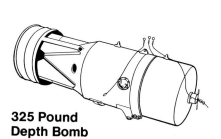

325 Pound Depth Bomb

1000 Pound GP Bomb

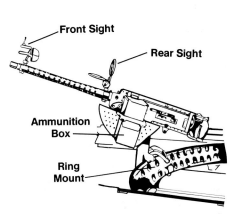

Front Sight

Rear Sight

Ammunition Box

Ring Mount

Browning .30 Caliber Machine Gun (SB2U-1/2)

During the many convoy escort missions conducted by USS RANGER in late 1941 and early 1942, the SB2U-2s of VS-41 operated primarily in the anti-submarine search role. (Navy via J.H. Weathers, Jr.)

Carrying two practice bomb dispensers in place of the wing bomb racks, an SB2U Vindicator of VS-41 High Hats conducts a training flight during 1942. The rear machine gun is in the stowed position. (Navy via W. F. Gemeinhardt)

This SB2U-2 of VS-41 (41-S-8) has the squadron's High Hat squadron insignia painted on the fuselage side just below the forward canopy section of the rear gunner's position. The framing around the pilot's canopy was natural metal. (Navy via W.L. Swisher)

Deck crews prepare to fold the wings of an SB2U-2 of VS-42 aboard RANGER during mid-1942. Wing folding was a manual operation and the worm gear jacks also doubled as braces once the wings were folded. The wings would be fully folded or left in a number of different semi-folded positions, depending on the space requirements at the time. (Navy via J.H. Weathers, Jr.)

With the wings partially folded, a pair of SB2U-2s of VS-42 are off-loaded from USS RANGER on 26 August 1942. Plane handlers push 42-S-14 clear so that the crane could lift the second aircraft, 42-S-8, from the hangar deck. (Navy via J.H. Weathers, Jr.)

Wing Fold System

Partially Folded

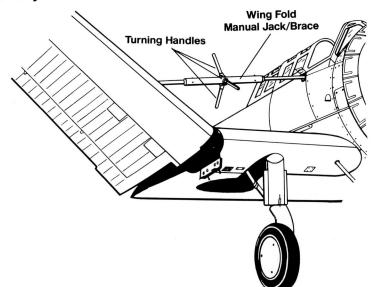

Turning Handles

Wing Fold
Manual Jack/Brace

Fully Folded

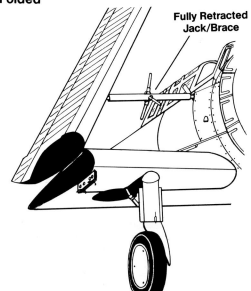

Fully Retracted
Jack/Brace

Seven SB2U-2 Vindicators of VS-41 enter the landing pattern for USS RANGER during Atlantic operations in 1942. Most of the aircraft are carrying a practice bomb dispenser under the port wing in place of the wing bomb rack. (National Archives via J.M. Elliott)

A flight deck crewman disengages the tailhook of this SB2U-2 Vindicator (42-S-4) of VS-42 from the arresting wire on USS RANGER in mid-1942. Once clear, the pilot will taxi forward to the aircraft's assigned parking spot. (National Archives)

The pilot and rear seat gunner exit this SB2U-2 (42-S-11) aboard RANGER after an anti-submarine patrol in mid-1942. The aircraft is armed with a depth bomb on the centerline bomb rack and has the aircraft number (11) painted on the nose and wing leading edge in White. (Navy via J.H. Weathers, Jr.)

An SB2U-2 Vindicator, 42-S-8, of Scouting Forty-two (VS-42) is craned off the hangar bay of USS RANGER on 26 August 1942. The aircraft is configured with a practice bomb dispenser under the port wing and a standard bomb rack under the starboard wing. (Navy via J.H. Weathers, Jr.)

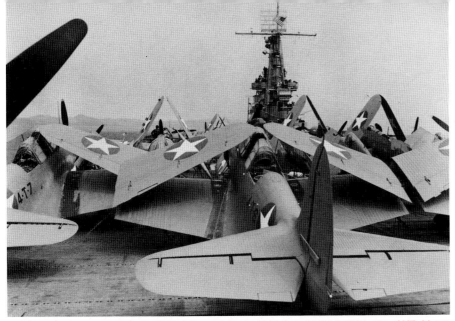

SB2U-2 Vindicators of VS-42, TBD-1 Devastators of VT-4 and F4F-3 Wildcats of VF-41 are tied down on the rear flight deck of USS RANGER while at anchor in Guantanamo Bay, Cuba on 18 June 1942. Each of the aircraft had a different wing fold arrangement. (National Archives)

The rear seat gunner waits on the Black wing walk of an SB2U-2 Vindicator of Scouting Squadron Forty-two (VS-42) on the flight deck of USS RANGER during August of 1942. (Navy via W. L. Swisher)

Combat at Midway

On 1 July 1941, Marine Scouting Squadron One (VMS-1) became Marine Scout-Bombing Squadron One Thirty-One (VMSB-131) under a new identification system that saw all other Marine Corps squadrons receiving new squadron identification numbers. The unit designation now identified the organizational structure of the unit: the designation VMSB-131 identified the squadron as belonging to the 1st Marine Air Wing (1), 3rd Marine Air Group (3) and the last 1 designated the unit as the 1st scout-bombing squadron with the Group.

VMSB-131 had been based at Quantico, Virginia during the pre-war years; however, after 7 December 1941 they were moved to the west coast with CAPT Paul Moret in command. Although they trained extensively in dive bombing techniques off the coast of San Diego during early 1942, when the squadron deployed to the Pacific rumors were already spreading that they were to become the first Grumman Avenger torpedo bomber squadron in the Marine Corps.

Deliveries of Grumman TBF-1 Avengers began on 24 September 1942 when the squadron received nine Avengers. By the time the squadron landed on Henderson Field, Guadalcanal on 12 November, all the SB2U-3s had all been replaced. During June of 1943 the squadron officially dropped the scout bombing title and became VMTB-131.

Just prior to the Japanese attack on Pearl Harbor, USS LEXINGTON had embarked eighteen SB2U-3s of VMSB-231 (of the twenty four aircraft assigned) for transportation to Midway Island. When the ship received word of the Japanese attack, she turned back and flew the SB2U-3s back to their base at Ewa. On arrival at MCAS Ewa, the squadron found that its remaining six SB2U-3s had been destroyed on the ground during the Japanese attack.

On 17 December 1941, the remaining airworthy SB2U-3s (seventeen aircraft) of VMSB-231 deployed from Ewa for the long overwater flight from Hawaii to Midway Island. Led by a PBY Catalina the unit set a new distance record for a flight of single engined aircraft. The squadron completed the 1,137 mile journey in 9 hours and 45 minutes, proving that the SB2U-3 had extremely "long legs."

The Vindicators joined the F2As of VMF-221 forming Marine Air Group 22. Shortly after their arrival at Midway, half of the squadron's personnel returned to MCAS Ewa where they became the cadre of a reorganized VMSB-231 and began transition training in the SBD-2 Dauntless. The unit at Midway, on 1 March 1942, was redesignated as VMSB-241 and took the squadron name, Sons of Satan. On 26 May, the squadron was reinforced by the arrival of nineteen SBD-2 Dauntless dive bombers which had been ferried to the island by the aircraft ferry USS KITTY HAWK. From that point on, the pilots flew training missions out over the Pacific near the island in preparation for action against the Japanese.

On the night of 3 June 1942, the Battle of Midway opened with an attack by Army Air Force B-17s and Navy PBYs against the Japanese troop ships of the Midway Occupation Force. The next morning, the Japanese launched 128 Zero fighters, Val dive bombers and Kate level bombers against Midway. At 0545 these aircraft were spotted by a patroling PBY that alerted Midway of the incoming Japanese strike.

First off in responce to the warning were the six TBF-1 Avengers of VT-8 followed by four Army B-26 Marauders. The second wave off the deck consisted of the sixteen SBD-2s of VMSB-241 led by MAJ Lofton R. Henderson the squadron's commandng officer. These were followed by a flight of seventeen B-17 Flying Fortress bombers. Last off were the twelve SB2U-3s. The Vindicators had simple orders — seek out and attack the approaching Japanese fleet. Shortly after takeoff, one of the SB2U-3s returned to Midway

Two SB2U-3s of VMSB-241 take off for a training flight shortly before the Battle of Midway. Vindicator number 6 (BuNo 2045) was flown on 4 June by 2LT James H. Marmande who was lost during the return to Midway Island. The rudder stripes have been overpainted with a fresh coat of Non-specular Blue Gray. (USMC via W. F. Gemeinhardt)

with mechanical problems while the eleven remaining SB2U-3s went on toward the Japanese. Each Vindicator was armed with a single 500 pound bomb on the centerline bomb rack.

The SBD element reached the Japanese ahead of the slower SB2U-3s and immediately attacked in a shallow glide bombing attack from 4,000 feet. Their target was the Japanese carrier HIRYU; however, the carrier's Combat Air Patrol was ready. MAJ Henderson was the first to be shot down by the Zero CAP. He was followed by five additional SBDs in only minutes. CAPT Richard E. Fleming (who was killed flying an SB2U-3 the next day) took over the lead and continued the attack on the HIRYU. Fleming and his gunner, CPL Eugene T. Card, managed to make their dive and drop their bomb, although their SB2U-2 was shot up and CPL Card was wounded in the attack. None of the SBDs scored a hit — eight were shot down and the rest were damaged.

The SBD divisions of VMSB-241 headed back to Midway as the SB2U-3s found the Japanese fleet, but they were on the opposite side of the fleet from the carriers. MAJ Benjamin W. Norris, flying the lead Vindicator, began a shallow dive from approximately 13,500 feet, followed by 2LT George T. Lumpkin and 2LT Kenneth O. Campion. Their target was the Japanese battleship HARUNA and Norris managed to score a near miss that caused some damage to the Japanese battleship.

Other SB2U-3s under MAJ Norris were intercepted by the Zero CAP. SGT Frank E. Zelnis, gunner aboard SB2U-3 #11 flown by 2LT Sumner H. Whitten, claimed one of the attacking A6M2 as destroyed. Other members of the squadron made runs on the Japanese ships, but VMSB-241 did not score any hits. Two SB2U-3s, one flown by 2LT Kenneth O. Campion and PVT. Anthony J. Maday (A/C #3) and another 2LT James H. Marmande and PFC Edby M. Colvin (A/C #6) failed to return and the cause of each disappearance is still unknown. Another SB2U-3, flown by 2LT Allan H. Ringblom, ran out of gas on the

return to Midway and ditched. Ringblom and his gunner, PVT Engine L. Webb, were rescued by PT-26, while PT-20 picked up LT Cummings who had ditched his Vindicator just a few miles short of Midway.

Later that day, VMSB-241 was again called upon to find and attack a Japanese carrier believed to be burning some 200 miles northwest of Midway. Six SBD-2s and six SB2U-3s took off at 1900 to search for the carrier. MAJ Norris lead the SB2Us and CAPT Marshall A. "Zack" Tyler lead the SBD-2s. The weather was bad in the search area and the target could not be located. On the return to Midway, MAJ Norris' Vindicator was seen to go into a steep right turn and disappeared. The rest of VMSB-241 made it to Midway safely.

At 0705 on 5 June, the remaining SBD-2s and SB2U-3s took off to find and attack the heavy cruisers, MIKUMA and MOGAMI, part of RADM Takeo Kurita's Cruiser Division 7.

CAPT Tyler's SBD group made a standard dive bombing attack but failed to hit their target, the MOGAMI. The SB2U-3 flight went in as glide bombers, attacking the MIKUMA. Fleming's plane was apparently hit at the start of the attack and bursted into flames. Neither Fleming nor his rear seat gunner, PFC George A. Toms escaped from the burning Vindicator. For his actions during the Battle of Midway, CAPT Fleming received the Congressional Medal of Honor, the first awarded to a Marine pilot in the Second World War. Later that day, Navy SBD dive bombers from the ENTERPRISE sank the MIKUMA and set the MOGAMI afire.

VMSB-241 was re-organized after the Midway battle and stayed on the island until March of 1943 when it rotated back to Hawaii. The squadron retained at least three of its SB2U-3s until September of 1943 as it transitioned to SBDs.

Marine Aircraft At Midway

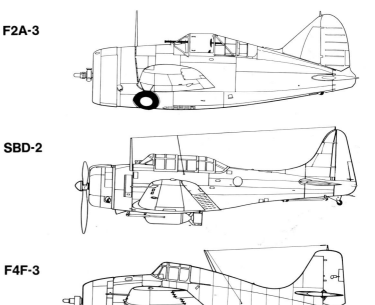

F2A-3

SBD-2

F4F-3

Japanese A6M Zero fighters flew combat air patrol (CAP) over the carriers at Midway and the Marine pilots quickly found out that the SB2U was clearly outmatched by the Zero.

Phase Out

On 1 March 1942, two Vindicator squadrons, VB-9 and VS-9 were commissioned at NAS Norfolk, Virginia as part of Carrier Air Group 9 (along with VF-9 and VT-9). The newly organized air group was scheduled to go aboard the USS ESSEX (CV-9) after the ship was commissioned in late December of 1942.

Both VS-9 and VB-9 received their first Vindicators during February of 1942 and by year's end, VS-9 had twelve SB2Us, while VB-9 had sixteen aircraft. During January 1943 both squadrons went aboard ESSEX and began work-up training operations. The SB2Us were in service aboard ESSEX for only a short period and by the end of February, VB-9 had departed ESSEX, prior to the ship's transit to the Pacific.

When VMSB-131 transitioned from the SB2U-3 to the TBF-1, the squadron turned over its Vindicators to VMSB-142 at Camp Kearny (San Diego) during September of 1942. By the end of that month, some of these aircraft were transferred once again, with

nine going to VMSB-143 and seven being delivered to VMSB-144. Toward the end of 1942, both squadrons were re-equipped with other types and transferred to the Pacific for combat operations.

The remaining SB2Us in the inventory were sent to various training units throughout the United States, ending their careers in the advanced training role. The longest record of operational service belongs to an SB2U-2 (BuNo 1330) which was retired on 30 November 1943.

No Vindicators survived the war, all having either been lost in action, training accidents or scrapped. One SB2U was reported last flown by Marine 2LT A.W. Lemmons. While operating from the Great Lakes training carrier, USS WOLVERINE, he reportedly ditched the Vindicator in Lake Michigan. Recently, the aircraft was successfully recovered from 130 feet of water and preliminary plans call for it to be restored and placed in the Naval Aviation Museum as a memorial for all the crews that flew the Vindicator, both in peace and war.

An SB2U-2 of VS-9 seconds away from engaging the Number 6 wire aboard USS CHARGER (AVG-30). The AVG designation was the original escort carrier designation that was given to all escort carriers until later, when the designation was changed to CVE. (Navy via J.H. Weathers, Jr.)

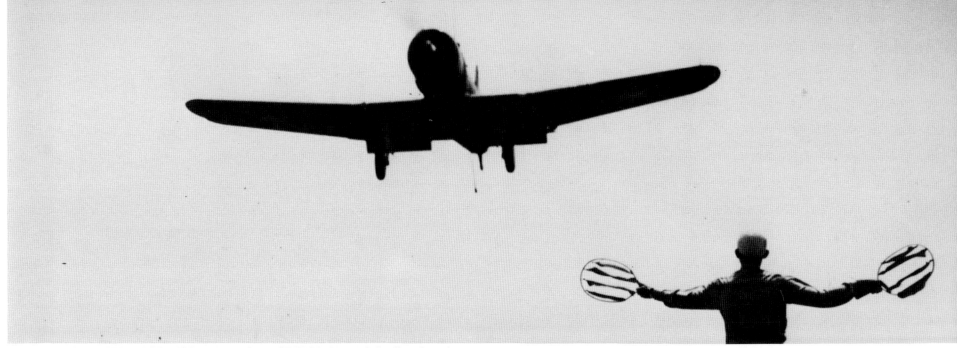

The Landing Signal Officer (LSO), LT Batters, guides an SB2U-2 in for a safe landing aboard USS CHARGER (AVG-30) during training operations on 10 July 1942. By this time the SB2U was being phased out of active squadrons and was used for advanced training. (Navy via J.H. Weathers, Jr.)

An SB2U-2 of VS-9 lands aboard USS CHARGER (ACV-30) on 29 October 1942. Air Group 9 was formed on 1 March 1942 for deployment aboard the new carrier USS ESSEX (CV-9). The ESSEX would not be commissioned until 31 December, so her Air Group trained aboard available carriers such as the CHARGER. (Navy via J.H. Weathers, Jr.)

This SB2U-1 Vindicator (BuNo 0778) of VB-9, flown by ENS R.A. Clarke, has dropped one wheel into the port catwalk aboard USS CHARGER during flight operations on 1 November 1942. By the time VB-9 was ready to go aboard ESSEX, the SB2Us were ready to be retired. (National Archives via J. H. Weathers, Jr.)

This SB2U-2 is about to cross the fantail of USS CHARGER and is just seconds from engaging an arresting wire. A number of SB2Us were used by the Training Command during the Summer and Fall of 1942. (Navy via J.H. Weathers, Jr.)

This SB2U-2 (9-S-18) of VS-9 aboard USS CHARGER during October of 1942 is unusual in that it carries a large fuselage star insignia forward on the fuselage. Normally SB2Us carried the insignia further back on the fuselage and was usually much smaller. (Navy via J.H. Weathers, Jr.)

SB2U-1. SB2U-2 and SB2U-3 Aircraft in Operational Service
1938-to 1943

Squadron Insignia	Carrier	Squadron Designation	1937	1938	1939	1940	1941	1942	1943
	LEXINGTON CV-2	VB-2		3/38	LEMON YELLOW TAILS		1/41		
	SARATOGA CV-3	VB-3	12/37 WHITE TAILS 1/39						
	RANGER CV-4	VB-3			1/39 7-1-39 GREEN				
	RANGER CV-4	VB-4			7-1-39 WILLOW GREEN TAILS 3-15-41				
	RANGER CV-4	VS-41					3-15-41 CAMOUFLAGE 9/42		
	RANGER CV-4	VB-4		12/38	1/39 GREEN				
	SARATOGA CV-3	VB-4			1/39 7-1-39 WHITE				
	SARATOGA CV-3	VB-3			2-1-39	WHITE	2-1-41 5/41 CAMO		
	RANGER CV-4	VS-42				12/40 GREEN	2-1-41 CAMOUFLAGE	3/42	
	WASP CV-7	VB-7				7/40 BLACK 11-15-40			
	WASP CV-7	VS-71					1/41 CAMOUFLAGE 5/42		
	WASP CV-7	VS-72			7-1-39	BLACK	2-1-41 CAMOUFLAGE	6/42	
	ESSEX CV-9	VB-9						3/42 CAMOUFLAGE 2/43	
	ESSEX CV-9	VS-9						2/42 CAMOUFLAGE 1/43	
	SARATOGA CV-3	VT-3			2/39 6/39 WHITE				
MARINE SQUADRONS									
	Quantico	VMS-1					5/41 7-1-41 CAMOUFLAGE		
	San Diego	VMSB-131* VMSB-143** VMSB-144***					* 7-1-41 CAMOUFLAGE 9/42	** 9/42 11/42 CAMO *** 9/42 12/42 CAMO	
	Ewa	VMS-2* VMSB-231**					* 3/41 7-1-41 GREY ** 7-1-41 CAMO	4/42	
	Camp Kearney	VMSB-142						9/42 10/42 CAMOUFLAGE	
	Midway Isl. 3-1-42	VMSB-241						4/42 6/42 CAMOUFLAGE	

49

More World War Two US Naval Aircraft
from squadron/signal publications

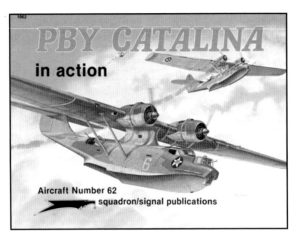

For a more complete listing of squadron/signal books, go to www.squadron.com